BIBLE
BANDS

CREATE YOUR OWN
FAITH-BASED RUBBER BAND JEWELRY

KATREINA EDEN

PLAIN SIGHT PUBLISHING
AN IMPRINT OF CEDAR FORT, INC.
SPRINGVILLE, UTAH

ACKNOWLEDGMENT

A SPECIAL THANKS to all my family members who helped in the writing process, in taking pictures, and in modeling the designs.

© 2014 Katreina Eden
All rights reserved.

ISBN 13: 978-1-4621-1505-1

Published by Plain Sight Publishing, an imprint of Cedar Fort, Inc.
2373 W. 700 S., Springville, UT 84663
Distributed by Cedar Fort, Inc., www.cedarfort.com

LIBRARY OF CONGRESS CATALOGING-IN-PUBLICATION DATA
Eden, Katreina, 1975- author.
Bible bands / Katreina Eden.
   pages cm
ISBN 978-1-4621-1505-1 (alk. paper)
1. Bible crafts. 2. Jewelry making. I. Title.

BS613.E34 2014
745.594'2--dc23
                              2014018266

Cover and page design by Angela D. Baxter
Cover design © 2014 by Lyle Mortimer
Edited by Daniel Friend

Printed in the United States of America

10 9 8 7 6 5 4 3 2 1

Printed on acid-free paper

1 INTRODUCTION

2 BASIC PATTERN

4 BASIC EXTENSION

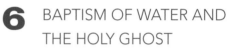

6 BAPTISM OF WATER AND THE HOLY GHOST

10 CHOOSE THE RIGHT

14 FAITH LIKE A MUSTARD SEED

18 GENEALOGY BRACELET

CONTENTS

22 GOD CREATED THIS BEAUTIFUL WORLD FOR ME

26 GOD LOVES ME

32 GOD'S PROMISE TO MANKIND

36 JOSEPH'S COAT OF MANY COLORS

40 LET YOUR LIGHT SHINE

44 LIVING WATERS OF EVERLASTING LIFE

48 LOVE ONE ANOTHER

52 ONE WITH GOD

56 STICK OF JUDAH AND STICK OF JOSEPH

60 ABOUT THE AUTHOR

III

INTRODUCTION

RUBBER BAND JEWELRY is fun to wear and even more fun to make. In this book, you'll not only learn cool jewelry designs but you'll also renew your appreciation to God for all the gifts He has given us. Each fun design is accompanied with a scripture from the Bible. Who says you can't have fun and give thanks to God at the same time?

BASIC PATTERN

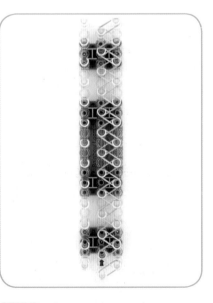

THE BASIC PATTERN is just to get you started on your rubber band jewelry journey. For the experts, it's a design you've seen before. I refer to it here because it's also used with other, more complicated designs throughout this book, and it gives those who are new to making rubber band jewelry a frame of reference. When placing the rubber bands, use your fingers. When looping the bands together, use the looping tool provided with your loom or use a crochet hook of similar size.

LOADING

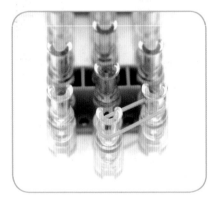

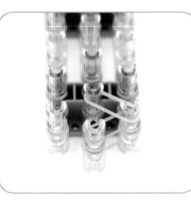

STEP 1 Be sure the open sides of the loom pins are facing away from you. Place a rubber band on the bottom center pin and stretch it diagonally to the bottom right pin.

STEP 2 Stretch another rubber band from the bottom right pin to the second center pin in another diagonal.

STEP 3 Follow this diagonal pattern all the way to the end of the loom.

LOOPING

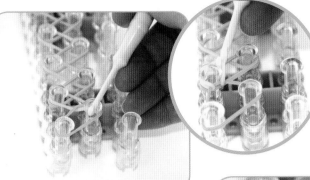

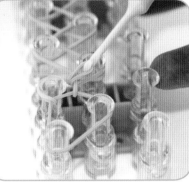

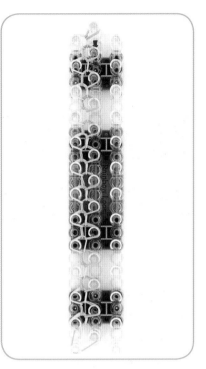

STEP 1 Turn the loom around so the open sides of the loom pins are facing toward you. Inserting the looping tool through the center of the open side of the loom pin, loop the bottom band of the bottom center pin to the pin where that band originated.

STEP 2 Loop the bottom band of the second-to-the-bottom pin on the left column to the pin where that band originated.

STEP 3 Continue this same looping pattern on every pin until you get to the end.

STEP 4 Attach a C-clip or S-clip to the top rubber band.

STEP 5 Slowly pull the bands off the loom

STEP 6 Attach the other end of the bracelet to your C- or S-clip to get your Basic Pattern bracelet.

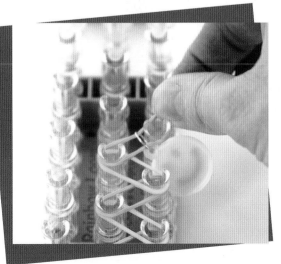

EXTRA!

WHEN ATTACHING a charm to any rubber band jewelry item, simply slide the rubber band through the charm hoop before stretching the band over the loom pins when loading the loom. Then, when you are looping, the charm will be securely attached like this

BASIC EXTENSION

THE BASIC EXTENSION is a simple pattern you can use when you want to make bracelets or necklaces longer without having to continue the bracelet or necklace pattern for the full length you want. This extension will be used throughout this book on various patterns.

STEP 1 When you've finished looping a design, move any outside bands to the center top pin so that all ending bands are on the same loom pin. (The open sides of the loom pins should already be facing you.)

STEP 2 Using your looping tool, pull a new band through the center of all the bands on the center loom pin. Then slide the tool's hook through both ends of the new band.

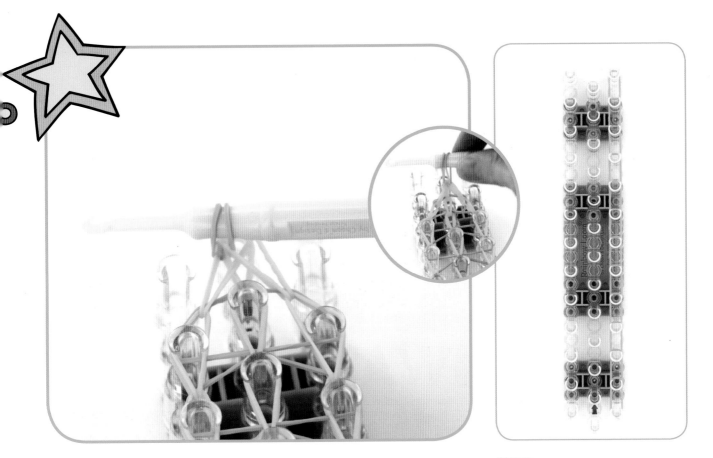

STEP 3 Move the new band to the indented section of the looping tool so it stays secure while you slowly pull the bracelet off the loom and set it aside.

STEP 4 With the loom pin openings facing away from you, place rubber bands straight down one side of the loom for the desired length as shown above.

STEP 5 Turn the loom around so the pin openings are facing you. Then, attach the band from the indented part of the looping tool to the top of the pin closest to you.

STEP 6 Loop the bottom band on that first pin around the pin directly above it, continuing this pattern all the way to the end of your extension.

STEP 7 Attach a C- or S-clip to the last band and slowly pull the extension off the loom. Attach the clip to the other end of your bracelet or necklace.

THE VOICE OF ONE crying in the wilderness, Prepare ye the way of the Lord, make his paths straight.

John did baptize in the wilderness, and preach the baptism of repentance for the remission of sins.

And there went out unto him all the land of Judæa, and they of Jerusalem, and were all baptized of him in the river of Jordan, confessing their sins.

And John was clothed with camel's hair, and with a girdle of a skin about his loins; and he did eat locusts and wild honey;

And preached, saying, There cometh one mightier than I after me, the latchet of whose shoes I am not worthy to stoop down and unloose.

Indeed have baptized you with water: but he shall baptize you with the Holy Ghost.

And it came to pass in those days, that Jesus came from Nazareth of Galilee, and was baptized of John in Jordan.

And straightway coming up out of the water, he saw the heavens opened, and the Spirit like a dove descending upon him:

And there came a voice from heaven, saying, Thou art my beloved Son, in whom I am well pleased.

MARK 1:3–11

BAPTISM OF WATER AND THE HOLY GHOST

WHEN WE ARE BAPTIZED,

we are cleansed of our sins. To represent this, this design uses blue for water and white for being clean. The colors are intertwined to represent immersion in water as Christ showed us when He was baptized. This design can also be done as a necklace or a ring. To make the bracelet, attach two looms together end to end to make one long loom.

LOADING

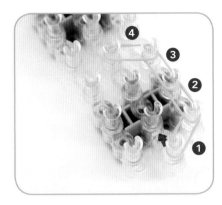

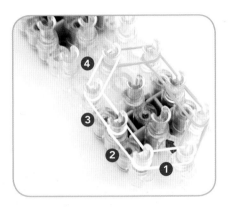

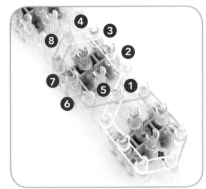

STEP 1 With the open sides of the loom pins facing away from you, place four blue rubber bands in a half-moon shape as shown.

STEP 2 Starting from the same bottom center pin again, place four white rubber bands in a half-moon shape going the other direction as shown.

STEP 3 Repeat the same half-moon pattern, starting from the center top pin where the last half-moon shapes met. This time, use the white rubber bands on the right side and the blue rubber bands on the left side as shown.

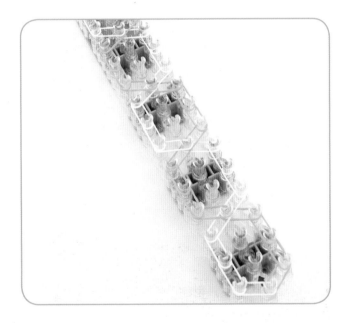

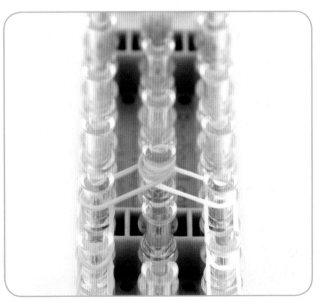

STEP 4 Repeat this same pattern as many times as needed to fit your wrist (or finger, if you're doing a ring), switching the blue and white rubber bands back and forth each time (most bracelets will only require one and a half loom lengths, or about six moon shapes, to fit your wrist). Each time, BE SURE to place the right side of the moon shape before placing the bands on the left side of the loom.

STEP 5 Add a triple-cap band to the center top loom pin. A triple- or double-cap band is simply looping one rubber band around the same loom pin three or two times. In this case, loop it three times to make a triple-cap band.

LOOPING

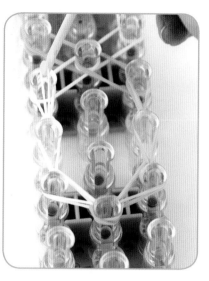

STEP 1 Turn the loom around so the open sides of the loom pins are facing you. Hook the band directly underneath the triple-cap band and loop it from the center pin up and to the right, onto the pin where it started.

STEP 2 Going back to the bottom center loom pin, loop the next band underneath the triple-cap band up and to the left, onto the pin where it started.

TIP: If you want to make a necklace, instead of adding a Basic Extension, simply loop the last top center loom pin bands around the looping tool and then pull all the bands off. Load an entire second section following steps 1–5 in the loading section above, but instead of placing a triple-cap band on the top center pin, simply place the bands that are around the looping tool to the top of that loom pin. Then follow steps 1–5 in the looping section. You can continue adding entire sections this same way until your necklace is as long as you want. When making a ring, you only need to use two of the full-moon sections.

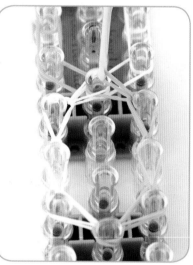

STEP 3 Loop the right and left sides of the oval straight up. When you come to the intersection, loop the left side of the moon onto the center column pin first. Then loop the right side.

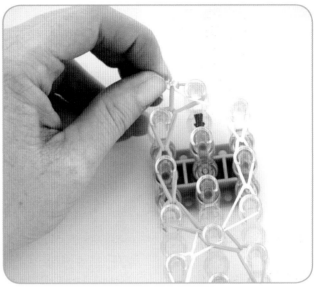

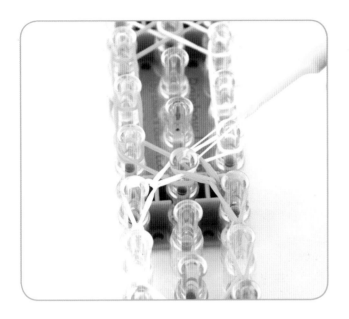

STEP 4 When looping from a center column intersection pin, always remember to loop the top band (just underneath the looped bands) BEFORE looping the bottom band.

STEP 5 Continue this same looping pattern all the way to the end. Then add a C- or S-clip or make a Basic Extension. Now you have cleanliness intertwined with the waters of baptism!

EXTRA!

YOU CAN ALSO use the dove charm from the Bible Charms Pack when making any of these items by following the directions in the EXTRA! section on page 3.

CHOOSE THE RIGHT

Now therefore fear the Lord, and serve him in sincerity and in truth: and put away the gods which your fathers served on the other side of the flood, and in Egypt; and serve ye the Lord.

And if it seem evil unto you to serve the Lord, choose you this day whom ye will serve; whether the gods which your fathers served that were on the other side of the flood, or the gods of the Amorites, in whose land ye dwell: but as for me and my house, we will serve the Lord.

JOSHUA 24:14–15

WE WERE GIVEN the gift of agency in this life to choose between right and wrong. Make this Choose the Right (CTR) bracelet to remind yourself to follow God and choose good. For this design, arrange the looms so there are four columns next to each other. Then attach four more columns to the top end so there are two four-column looms placed end-to-end (see images in the Loading section for loom setup).

BECAUSE THIS PATTERN forms letters with the rubber bands, you'll need to follow the layout of the two colors precisely, though you may use any two colors of your choosing. Whenever you place the black bands (or letter bands), double up—use two bands for every loop. This will make the letters thicker and easier to see when your bracelet is done.

LOADING

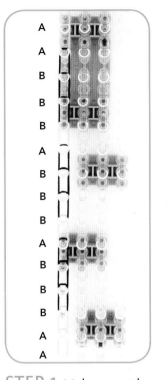

A
A
B
B
B
A
B
B
B
A
B
B
B
A
A

STEP 1 Make sure the open sides of the loom pins are facing away from you. On the far left loom column, starting at the bottom, place two different colors of rubber bands in the order shown in the diagram. Go straight up. You will use six aqua (A) bands and eighteen black (B) bands (nine loops with two bands each).

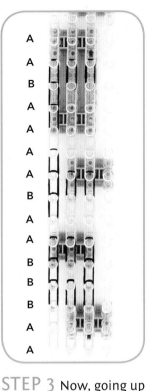

A
A
B
A
A
A
A
B
A
A
B
A
B
A
A

STEP 2 Going straight up the second loom column from the left, place your two different colors of rubber bands as indicated in the diagram. You will use eleven aqua bands and eight black bands.

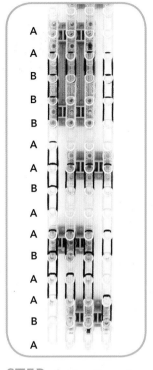

A
A
B
A
A
A
A
B
A
B
B
A
A

STEP 3 Now, going up the third loom column from the left, place the bands as shown in the diagram. You will use ten aqua bands and ten black bands.

A
A
B
B
B
A
A
A
A
A
B
A
A
B
A

STEP 4 Finally, going up the right-hand loom column, place the bands as shown in the diagram. You will use nine aqua bands and twelve black bands.

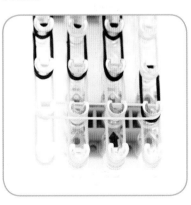

STEP 5 Now, starting with the second row of loom pins from the bottom, place an aqua rubber band around the entire row of loom pins as shown. Be sure to push all the bands down so there is still room at the top of the pin for looping.

STEP 6 Continue this straight-across pattern with the aqua bands until you get to the end of the rows with rubber bands.

LOOPING

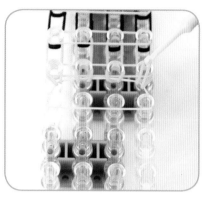

STEP 1 Turn the loom around so that the open sides of the loom pins are facing you. Starting with the bottom of the far left loom column, loop the bottom aqua band straight up onto the pin above it in the left column (the straight-across row bands are left alone).

STEP 2 Do the same with the second column from the left, looping the bottom aqua band straight up onto the next pin in that same column.

STEP 3 In the same fashion, loop the bottom aqua bands on the third and fourth columns onto the pins above them.

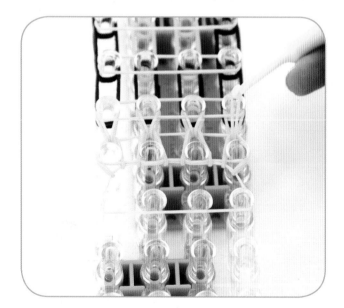

STEP 4 Repeat steps 1–3 on the next row up, starting from the leftmost pin.

STEP 5 Moving to the far left column on the third row up, loop the doubled-up black bands by pulling both bands at the same time straight up onto the next pin in that same column.

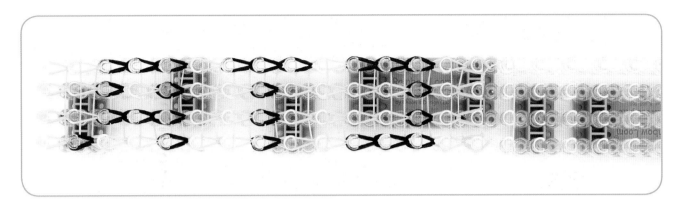

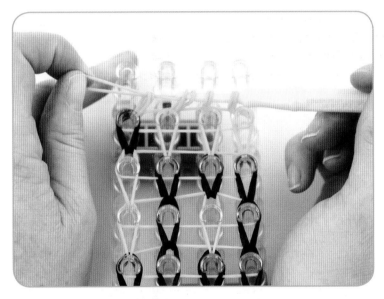

STEP 6 Continue this same looping pattern row by row in each column until you reach the top of the loom (the straight-across row bands are left alone).

EXTRA!

FOR A THINNER bracelet, you can use the CTR charm from the Bible Charms Pack with the simple Basic Pattern by following the steps in the EXTRA! section on page 3.

STEP 7 Finish the bracelet by adding a Basic Extension and C-clip. Doing the Basic Extension with four loops at the end of the loom instead of three can be a bit tricky. To do this, simply loop the two outside loops to the two center loops. Then place the two center loops onto the looping tool one at a time, sliding them down past the indent to keep them from coming off. Next, place one aqua rubber band on the end hook and turn the hook so it is facing the bracelet. Slowly pull that band through the rest of the loops. Be sure to hold the other end of that aqua band with your fingers when you pass it through all the bracelet loops so that you can connect the two ends as described in the Basic Extension pattern. From here, you simply continue with the Basic Extension pattern. Now, turn your bracelet over, and WALA! You have spelled C-T-R to remind yourself to choose the right when choices are hard.

FAITH IS LIKE A MUSTARD SEED

DID YOU KNOW that the mustard seed is one of the smallest seeds on Earth? One mustard seed can grow into a plant 15 feet tall and 15 feet wide. Christ teaches us that if we have the smallest faith, like a mustard seed, and we exercise it, it can grow into great faith. This design plants several "mustard seeds" around the bracelet to remind you to exercise your faith.

BEFORE PLACING THE rubber bands, move the left loom pin column down a notch so it is parallel with the center column, but keep the right column up one notch at a diagonal as shown.

LOADING

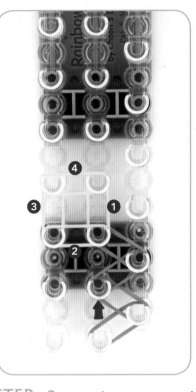

STEP 1 Start by placing four gray rubber bands in the Basic Pattern on the right and center columns, making sure the open sides of the loom pins are facing away from you.

STEP 2 On the center and left columns, place four yellow rubber bands in a square. Be sure to add them in the exact number order shown in the diagram. This is your "mustard seed" section.

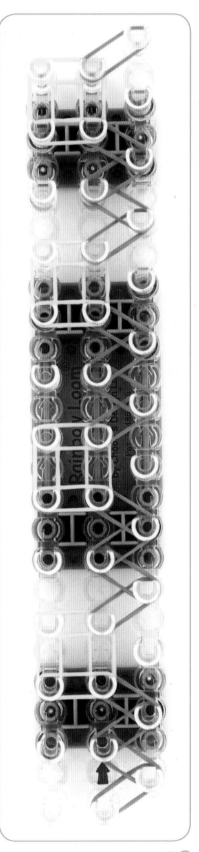

STEP 3 Continue with four gray rubber bands in the Basic Pattern on the right and center columns of the loom. Then repeat the mustard seed section using the center and left columns of the loom. Continue to repeat these two sections until you have your jewelry as long as you want it (connect looms end-to-end when making longer jewelry).

LOOPING

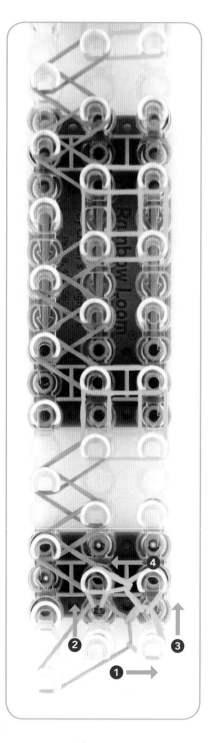

STEP 1 To begin looping, turn the loom around so the open sides of the loom pins are facing you. Depending on how long you made your jewelry, you will start looping either a Basic Pattern section or a mustard seed section.

TIP: To make a ring, just create one mustard seed section with one and a half Basic Pattern sections.

STEP 2 When looping a mustard seed section, be sure to loop it in the exact order shown in the diagram. When looping a Basic Pattern, refer back to the Basic Pattern section on page 3.

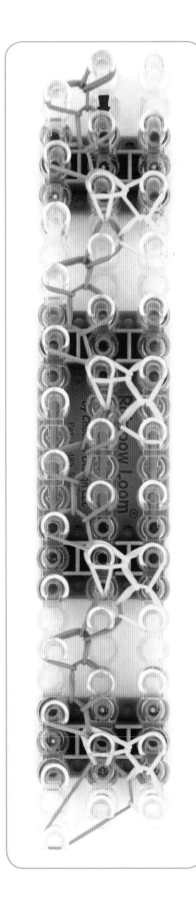

STEP 3 Continue this looping pattern until you reach the end. Be sure you have looped the final rubber band. Then attach a C-clip or S-clip to the top rubber band and slowly pull the rubber bands off the loom. Now you have little yellow "mustard seeds" that go all the way around your bracelet or necklace.

GENEALOGY BRACELET

AS STATED IN Malachi, God has commanded us to seek out our fathers, or in other words, our ancestors. We turn our hearts to our fathers by doing our genealogy. All over the world, people of all faiths are researching their genealogy, trying to find all their family members. This bracelet connects rings of color from one generation to the next, representing the connection of family through time. For this design, you will want to connect two looms from top to bottom and make the columns square (similar to the Choose the Right design, but this time use three columns instead of four).

LOADING

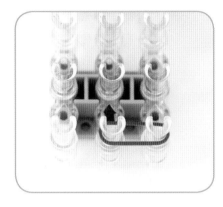

STEP 1 With the open sides of the loom pins facing away from you, place one band across the bottom right and center pins.

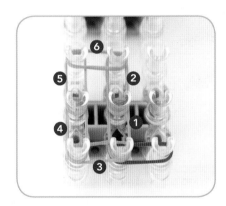

STEP 2 Using a different color, place six rubber bands in a rectangle shape in the order shown above.

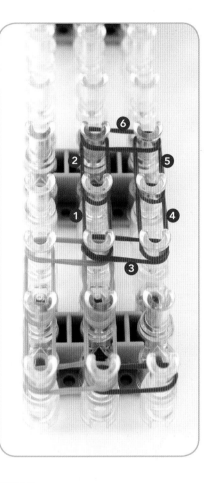

STEP 3 Using a third color, follow this same pattern on the right side of the loom, placing six rubber bands in another rectangle.

STEP 4 Follow this same pattern all the way up the length of two looms, using a different color for each rectangle and moving back and forth from the left side to the right side and so on. Be sure to stop with your last full rectangle, which will leave the top row of the loom pins empty. These rectangles will turn into circles after you loop them and pull them off the looms.

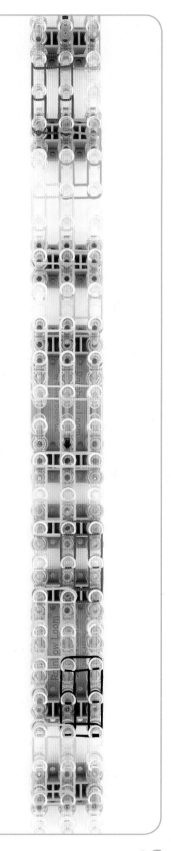

LOOPING

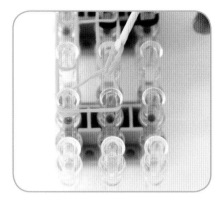

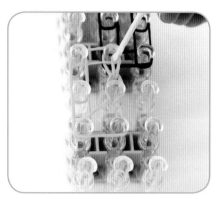

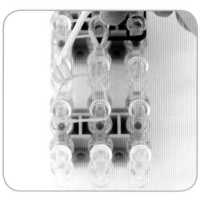

STEP 1 To start looping, turn the loom around so the open sides of the loom pins are facing you. Start with the bottom band on the center pin. Loop the band straight up onto its starting pin.

STEP 2 Loop the band from the next pin in the center column straight up as well.

STEP 3 Loop the band on the bottom pin in the left-hand column straight up onto its starting pin.

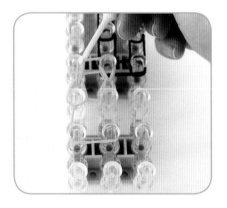

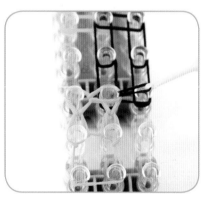

STEP 4 Loop the band from the next pin in the left-hand column straight up as well.

STEP 5 Now, starting in the left column at the top of the rectangle, loop the band from the left row pin to the pin directly to its right.

STEP 6 Continue straight across by looping the second-to-the-bottom band on the center pin you ended on in step 5 directly to the right, to the pin where it started.

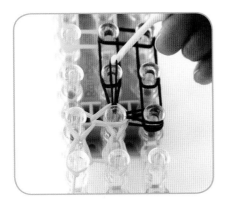

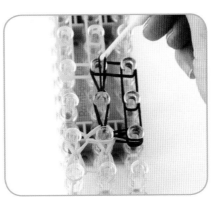

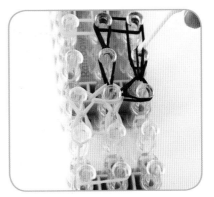

STEP 7 Going back to the center pin, loop the remaining bottom band straight up to the pin where it started.

STEP 8 Continuing straight up the center column, loop the next center row band straight up to the next pin.

STEP 9 Going down to the bottom right corner of the rectangle, loop the band in the right column straight up to the pin where it started.

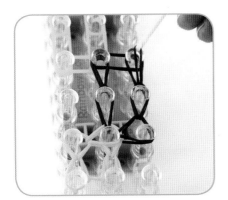

STEP 10 Loop the band from the next pin in the right column straight up as well.

STEP 11 Follow this same pattern from steps 1–10 all the way to the top of the looms.

STEP 12 Attach a C- or S-clip to the last rubber band loop and slowly pull the bracelet off the loom. Now you have a beautiful bracelet of family circles connecting through the generations.

GOD CREATED THIS BEAUTIFUL WORLD FOR ME

DURING THE SIX days of creation, God made a beautiful world for us to live in. This design creates a sun in the center of a modified Basic Pattern to represent the source of life and light upon this earth.

LOADING

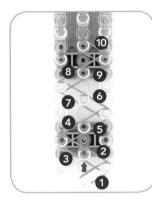

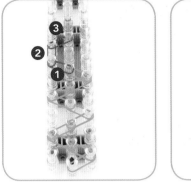

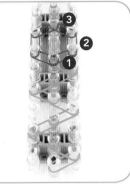

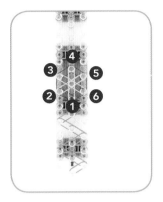

STEP 1 With the open sides of the loom pins facing away from you, start by placing ten green bands (representing grass) in the order shown. This is basically a wider Basic Pattern that utilizes all three columns instead of two. This will make the bracelet longer on each side of the sun.

STEP 2 To represent the sun, use three different colors of flame (yellow in the middle as the hottest, then orange, and then red). Start by placing three orange bands in a half-circle pattern on the left side as shown.

STEP 3 Place the right half of the circle, starting at the bottom and going to the right as shown.

STEP 4 Place the six yellow bands of the flame in a spoke pattern, starting from the bottom pin of the sun circle and going to the empty center pin. Move clockwise to place the other yellow bands.

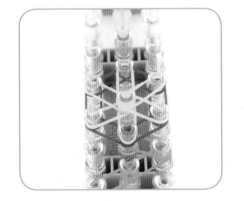

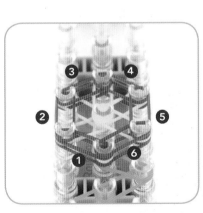

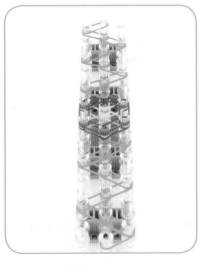

STEP 5 In the very center of the sun pattern, place a yellow triple-cap band.

STEP 6 Now, with the final outside color of the flame (red), place six red bands in a circle, starting with the bottom pin of the sun pattern and moving clockwise until you reach the bottom pin again.

STEP 7 Starting on the top center pin of the sun pattern, continue the widened Basic Pattern shown in step 1. Use ten green bands, and you will reach the top center pin of the loom.

LOOPING

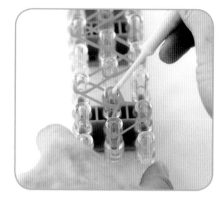

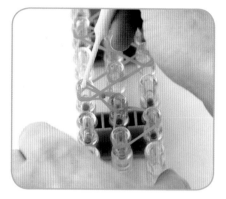

STEP 1 To start looping, turn the loom around so the open sides of the pins are facing you. Then, start looping from the second-to-the-bottom pin in the right column, looping the band onto the pin where it started.

STEP 2 Continuing from the center pin where step 1 ended, loop the bottom band up diagonally to the pin in the left column where it started.

STEP 3 From that pin, loop the bottom band up diagonally to the center column pin where it started.

STEP 4 Continue this looping pattern (the same as the Basic Pattern) until you reach the bottom of the sun pattern.

STEP 5 When looping the sun pattern, start in the very center with the pin that has the cap band. Looping the looping tool through the center of the cap band, pull the top band underneath the cap band up and loop it onto the pin where it originated (up diagonally to the left).

STEP 6 Continue looping the yellow bands back to the pins they started from. Go in a counter-clockwise direction. (The last one in line underneath the cap band will go to the bottom-left peg in the sun pattern). BE SURE you always put the looping tool through the center of the cap band to grab each yellow band.

STEP 7 Now, starting at the bottom center pin of the sun pattern, loop the top orange band (the second band to the bottom) up and to the left diagonally, to the loom pin where it started.

STEP 8 From that pin, loop the bottom orange band straight up to the pin where it started.

STEP 9 From that pin, loop the bottom orange band diagonally to the right, to the pin where it started.

TIP: To make a sun ring, you'll only need two or three of the regular (not widened) Basic Pattern rubber bands on each side of the sun pattern.

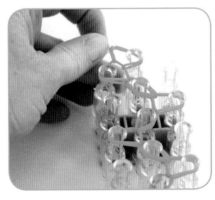

EXTRA!

STEP 10 Now, going back to the bottom center pin of the sun pattern, loop the bottom orange band up and to the right diagonally. Continue the same looping pattern with the orange bands on this side as you did on the left side (the red bands are left alone and are not looped).

STEP 11 Starting on the top center pin of the sun pattern, continue looping the remaining green rubber bands of the Basic Pattern as you did in steps 1–4. Place a C- or S-clip on the last band and slowly pull the bands off the loom. Now you have a sun in the middle of green grass!

YOU CAN ALSO use the Earth, Sun, or Butterfly charms from the Bible Charms Pack on the grass part of the bracelet by following the steps in the EXTRA! section on page 3.

GOD LOVES ME

EVERY BLESSING WE have—the world we live in, the scriptures, our friends, our families, even the air we breathe—is an evidence of God's love for us. This triple-heart bracelet will help remind you of God's love for you.

LOADING

LOOPING

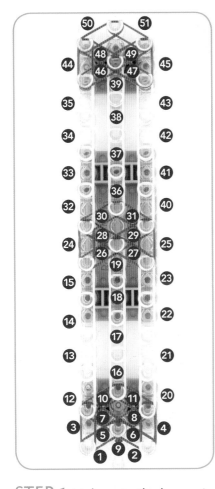

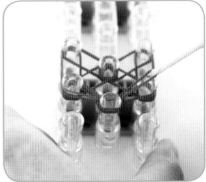

STEP 1 Make sure the loom pin openings are facing away from you. Place white and red (or pink) rubber bands on the loom in the order shown in the photo.

STEP 1 Turn the loom around so the loom pin openings are facing toward you. Then, starting on the bottom pin in the center column, use the looping tool to loop the first band underneath the cap band onto the pin where it started.

STEP 2 Going back to the bottom pin in the center column, loop the bottom band onto the pin where it started.

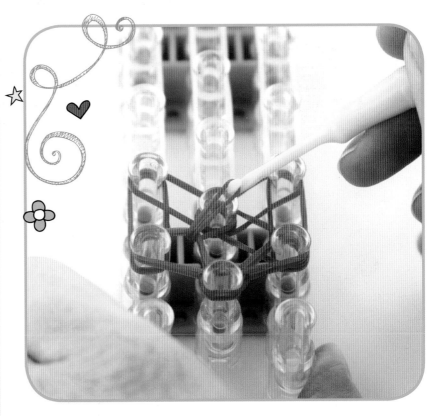

STEP 2 Place one red (or pink) triple-cap band at the very top center loom pin. This will be the bottom point of a heart.

STEP 3 From the second-to-the-bottom pin in the left column, loop the second-to-the-bottom band onto the center column pin where it started.

LOOPING

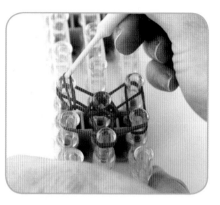

STEP 4 From the second-to-the-bottom pin in the right column, loop the second-to-the-bottom band onto the center column pin where it started.

STEP 5 Going back to the second-to-the-bottom pin in the left column, loop the bottom band straight up onto the pin where it started.

STEP 6 Now, on the second-to-the-bottom pin in the right-hand column, loop the bottom band straight up onto the pin where it started.

STEP 7 From the second-to-the-bottom pin in the center column, loop the third-to-the-bottom band onto the pin where it started.

STEP 8 Going back to the second-to-the-bottom pin in the center column, loop the second-to-the-bottom band onto the pin where it started. At this point, only the red (or pink) bands should have been looped.

STEP 9 Starting with the top left corner of the heart, loop the white band straight up onto the pin where it started.

STEP 10 Continue looping the white bands in the left column straight up until you reach the next heart section.

STEP 11 Starting with the second pin from the bottom in the center column, loop the white band straight up onto the pin where it started.

STEP 12 Continue looping the white bands in the center column straight up until you reach the next heart section.

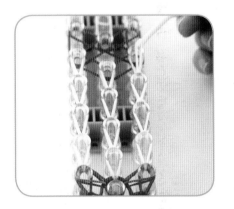

STEP 13 Follow this same looping pattern for the white bands in the right column.

STEP 14 Follow the looping pattern from steps 1–8 for the second heart pattern. Start with the bottom center point of the heart.

STEP 15 Follow the looping pattern from steps 9–13 for the next set of white bands. Start with the left column.

LOOPING

STEP 16 Once again, follow the looping pattern from steps 1–8 for the heart pattern. Remember to start with the bottom center pin.

STEP 17 Loop the band from the top pin in the left column to the top center pin.

STEP 18 Loop the band from the second-to-the-top pin in the center column straight up to the top center pin.

STEP 19 Loop the band from the top pin in the right column to the top center pin.

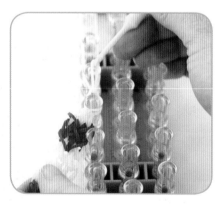

STEP 20 Follow the Basic Extension pattern at the beginning of the book to finish the bracelet.

STEP 21 SPECIAL NOTE: Instead of attaching a C- or S-clip to the triple-cap band end of the bracelet, simply use your looping tool to pull a new band through the cap band as shown. Then attach a C- or S-clip to this new band. Now you have a lovely triple-heart bracelet.

TIP: To make matching drop-heart earrings, simply make one heart pattern as shown and then add a Basic Extension of just three or four white bands. Attach an earring hook to the top white band. To make a matching heart pendant necklace, make one heart pattern with one section of straight white bands up all three columns. Connect them in the center and then continue with two Basic Patterns from this point to make the necklace chain. Try alternating red (or pink) and white bands with the Basic Pattern to add extra color to your chain.

GOD'S PROMISE TO MANKIND

EVERYBODY LOVES rainbows. They are the magic that happens when light and water are mixed together. But did you know that God gave us the rainbow as a symbol of a promise? After Noah and his family set foot on dry ground, God promised that He wouldn't flood the earth again. Every time we see a rainbow, we can think of God's promise to us. We can do the same whenever we see our rainbow rubber band jewelry. Just follow these simple steps to create a colorful bracelet, necklace, anklet, ring, or earrings. For those of you who have seen the fishbone design, this design will be familiar to you.

THIS DESIGN USES two loom pins next to each other. It doesn't matter if the open side of the loom pins is facing to the right or to the left. Even though the images show the open sides of the loom pins facing right, it can also be done with the open sides facing left. Follow the steps below, remembering your rainbow colors: ROYGBIV (Red, Orange, Yellow, Green, Blue, Indigo, and Violet). Indigo is a very dark blue that's almost purple, so make sure it looks darker than your blue and violet bands.

LOADING AND LOOPING

STEP 1 Start by twisting a red band into a figure eight onto two neighboring pins.

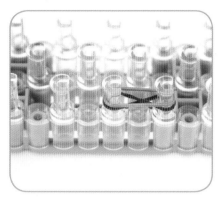

STEP 2 Place an orange band on top of the red band. (Do not twist the orange band into a figure eight).

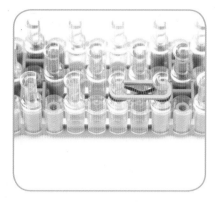

STEP 3 Place a yellow band on top of the orange band.

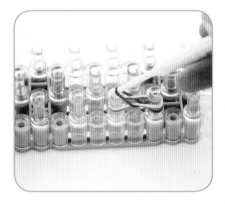

STEP 4 Take the red (bottom) band on the left pin and loop it to the center over the other two bands. (Notice that for this design, you are looping the bands over the OUTSIDE of the pins rather than through the middle.)

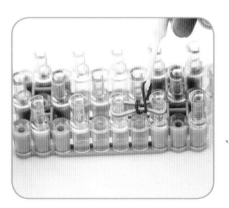

STEP 5 Do the same on the other side—take the red band on the right pin and loop it to the center over the other two bands.

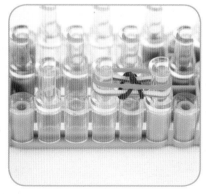

STEP 6 Place a green band straight on top of the other bands.

LOADING AND LOOPING

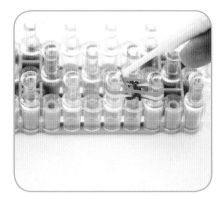

STEP 7 Now, follow the instructions in step 4, only with the orange (bottom) band–take the orange band on the left pin and loop it to the center over the other two bands.

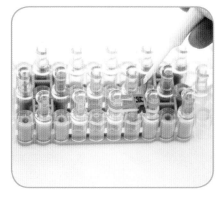

STEP 8 Do the same with the orange band on the right pin.

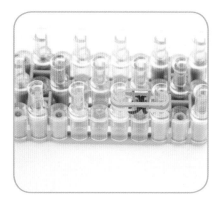

STEP 9 Place a blue band on top of the other bands. Nudge the bands down as you go to make room for each new band.

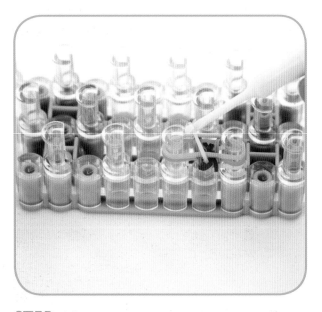

STEP 10 Follow the instruction as in steps 4 and 7 with the yellow (bottom) band, looping the yellow band on the left pin to the center over the other two bands.

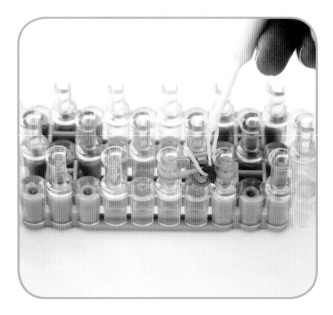

STEP 11 Do the same with the yellow band on the right pin.

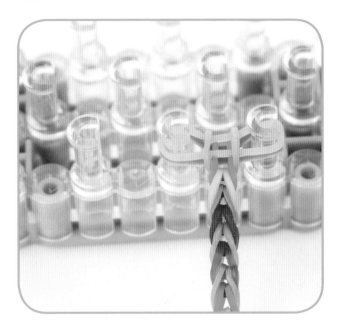

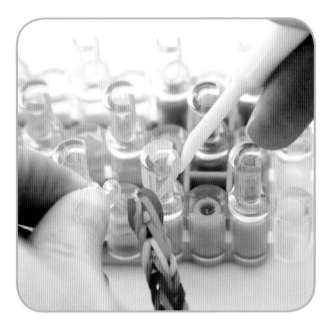

STEP 12 Continue to follow these same steps with each additional color. You can make the rainbow as long as you like. Because the design forms off the side of the loom, you can measure the length as you go to make it fit your wrist, ankle, finger, or neckline. You can also make a set of straight earrings by looping two full sets of ROYGBIV colors and attaching an earring hook to the top color.

STEP 13 When the rainbow is long enough, simply loop the bottom band to the center on both the left and right side. This should leave just one band left on the pins. Take the left and right sides of that band and attach a C- or S-clip to them as shown. Congratulations! Now you have completed a rainbow reminding you of God's promise.

TIP: Use several bands of the same color in a row to make a thicker-looking rainbow. For example, use three red bands, then three orange bands, then three yellow bands, and so on.

EXTRA!

YOU CAN ALSO use the Noah's Ark or the Rainbow charm from the Bible Charms Pack when making any of these items simply by following the directions in the EXTRA! section on page 3.

JOSEPH'S COAT OF MANY COLORS

JOSEPH WAS SOLD into Egypt as a slave by his brothers. But later, with God's help, and because he was in Egypt, Joseph was able to save not only his family from a seven-year famine but all of the people in the land as well. Joseph is a great example to us of rising above difficulties and trials no matter how hard they may be. This fun, colorful bracelet will help remind you that with God's help, you can rise above the hard times in your life.

LOADING

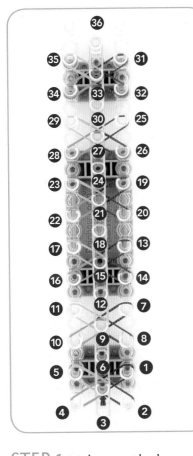

STEP 1 Make sure the loom pin openings are facing away from you. Then place the colored bands in the order shown in the image.

STEP 2 Place a white triple-cap band on the top pin in the center column as well as on the pin in the center of each wheel of color.

LOOPING

STEP 1 Turn the loom around so the loom pin openings are facing toward you. Then, use the looping tool to grab the purple band underneath the white cap band on the bottom pin of the center column. Loop the purple band straight up onto the pin where it started.

STEP 2 From the center of the color wheel, loop the top band underneath the cap band onto the pin where it started. (This should be the blue band.)

STEP 3 From the center of the color wheel, loop the next band underneath the cap band onto the pin where it started. (This should be the green band.)

LOOPING

STEP 4 Continue in a counter-clockwise direction, looping from the center of the color wheel until the entire wheel has been looped.

STEP 5 Moving to the center column, loop the purple band that connects the two color wheels straight up onto the pin where it started.

STEP 6 Following the looping pattern in steps 2-4, loop the next color wheel. Continue this looping pattern until all the color wheels are connected and looped.

STEP 7 Before taking the bands off the loom, add another band of the same color to the outside pins of each color wheel. To do so, place the looping tool down through the pin opening and through the looped band. Then pull the new band up through the opening (similar to step 2 of the Basic Extension).

STEP 8 Loop one end of this added band through itself. Pull it tight in a slipknot, sliding it to center of the looped band.

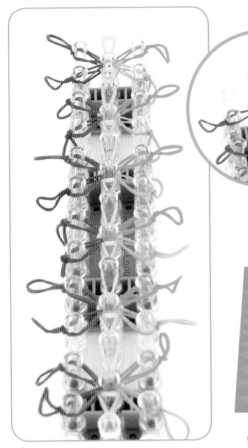

EXTRA!

YOU CAN ALSO use the Multicolored Flower charm from the Bible Charms Pack when making this bracelet by following the instructions in the EXTRA! section on page 3.

TIP: For a longer bracelet, connect two looms end to end and continue the color wheel pattern for as long as you want.

STEP 9 Once you have added a new band to each of the outside pins of each color wheel (these should be the green, blue, red, and orange bands), add a C- or S-clip to the top yellow band in the center column and slowly pull the bands off the loom. Then, connect the C- or S-clip to the other side of the bracelet. (If you don't want to attach the clip to the cap band on the other end, simply pull an extra band through the cap band using your looping tool and then attach the clip to that band.)

LET YOUR LIGHT SHINE

WHEN WE HAVE been blessed with God's love and light, we feel happiness and want to share it with everyone around us. With this snazzy bracelet, ring, or hair accessory, you can let your light shine to spread happiness around you.

LOADING

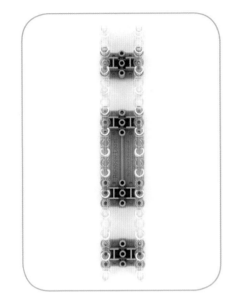

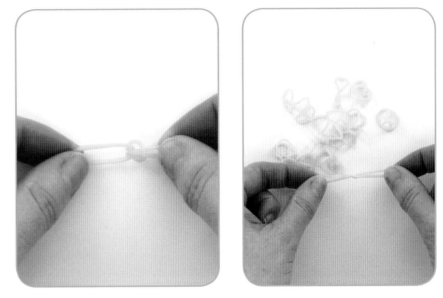

STEP 1 Remove the center column of loom pins from your loom so that you have two columns with a space between them as shown.

STEP 2 Tie two rubber bands together in a slipknot and pull tight. Do this with 30 bands, creating 15 sets of tied bands.

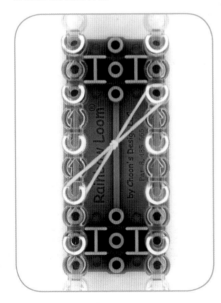

STEP 3 Be sure the open sides of the loom pins are facing away from you. Place one tied set of bands on the pins, crossing the center as shown. Be sure to skip one row of pins to pull your band tighter.

STEP 4 Place another tied set of bands crossing in the other direction, skipping one row of pins as before. Your two sets of tied bands should form an X.

STEP 5 Continue repeating steps 3 and 4 until all the tied sets of bands are placed on the loom. You will need to push bands down toward the bottom of the pins in order to fit all the bands. It is easiest to do this each time you place a new tied set.

LOOPING

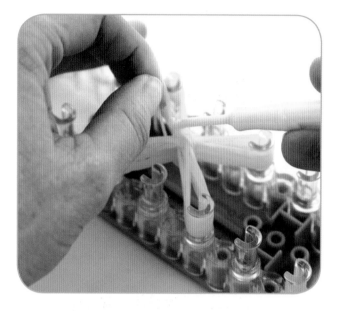

STEP 1 Take a single rubber band and wrap it around the center of the X. Loop one end of the band through the other and pull tight. Then attach a C-clip to the end that you have pulled tight.

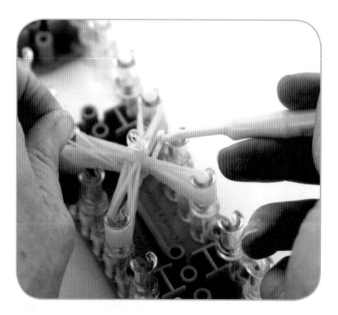

STEP 2 Take another single band and do the same thing as step 1, but do so going the other direction on the X. Attach it to another C-clip.

STEP 3 Remove all the bands from the loom. Cut through the four loops of the X, taking care not to cut the center two bands. Now you have your fluffy ball of light! Attach your ball of light to a ring, bracelet, or hair accessory. You can also stack more than 15 sets of tied bands to make an even fluffier ball.

TIP: Use glow-in-the-dark rubber bands on the light ball for even more fun in the dark!

LIVING WATERS OF EVERLASTING LIFE

JESUS TEACHES US that by drinking the water He gives us, or in other words, living His teachings as found in the scriptures, we will never thirst and will gain eternal life with Him. You can make a bracelet of flowing water out of rubber bands to remind yourself to partake daily from the Word of God.

LOADING

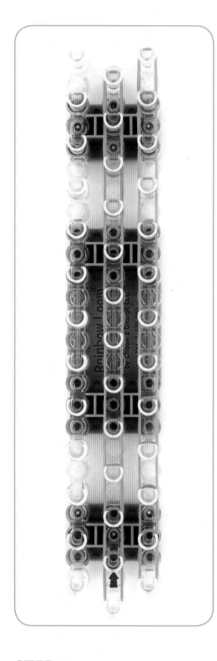

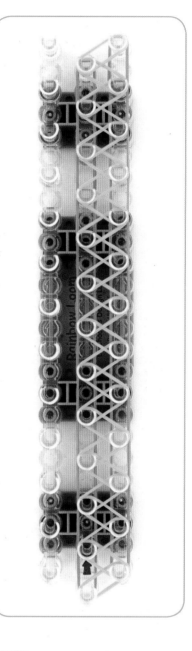

STEP 2 Using light blue rubber bands, weave the bands back and forth, starting with the center bottom loom pin and going up to the right, then going from that pin up to the center with another band, and so on. This is just like the Basic Pattern.

STEP 1 With the open sides of the loom pins facing away from you, place dark blue rubber bands in a straight line down the center column. Then, place dark blue rubber bands in a straight line down the right-hand column just as you did in the center column.

STEP 3 Continue this zigzag pattern all the way to the end of the loom.

LOOPING

STEP 1 For looping, turn your loom around so the open sides of the loom pins are facing you. Then, starting with the bottom left-hand loom pin, loop the dark blue rubber band straight up to the pin where it started.

STEP 2 Moving to the center column, once again loop the dark blue rubber band straight up to the pin where it started.

STEP 3 Going back to the bottom loom pin in the center column, loop the light blue rubber band up and to the left diagonally to the pin where it started.

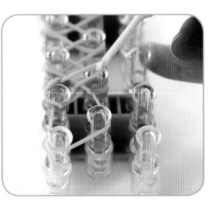

STEP 4 Moving to the second loom pin from the bottom in the left column, loop the dark blue rubber band straight up just as in step 1.

STEP 5 Going back to the second loom pin on the left column again, loop the light blue rubber band up and to the right diagonally to the pin where it started.

STEP 6 Moving to the second loom pin to the bottom in the center column, loop the dark blue rubber band straight up as in step 1.

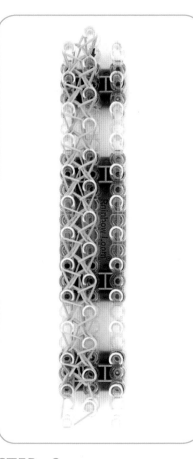

STEP 7 Going back again to the second loom pin in the center column, loop the light blue rubber band up and to the left diagonally to the pin where it started.

STEP 8 Continue this same looping pattern from steps 2–7, remembering to loop the dark blue rubber band straight up on each loom pin before looping the light blue rubber band in the zigzag pattern. BE SURE to loop both rubber bands on each pin before moving to the next pin.

STEP 9 IMPORTANT STEP: When you get the end, use your hook tool to reach down through all the loops around the top pin in the center column. Then loop down through the BOTTOM dark blue rubber band on the top pin in the left column.

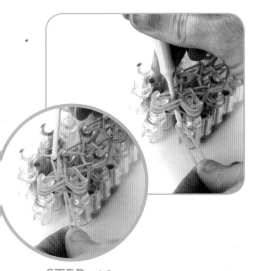

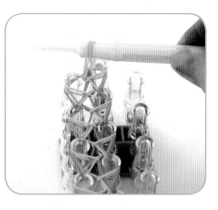

STEP 10 Attach a new light blue rubber band to the hook and slowly pull one end through all the loops, making sure to hold on to the other end.

STEP 11 Now, slide the looping tool through the other end of that light blue rubber band and move the band to the indented part of the looping tool to prevent the band from falling off the end.

Slowly pull the bracelet off the loom and attach the ends together with a C- or S-clip, or add a Basic Extension. Now you can see the ripples of different colors of water moving through the bracelet.

 47

LOVE ONE ANOTHER

GOD WANTS US to be kind to one another and love all people. This beautiful mini-hearts bracelet or necklace will remind you to do just that. For this design, you will need to make your loom square (move the center column so that all the columns are even).

LOADING

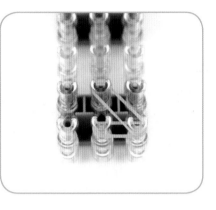

STEP 1 Make sure the open sides of the loom pins are facing away from you. Start by placing a purple band on the two bottom right pins as shown.

STEP 2 Stretch a purple band diagonally from the bottom right pin to the second-row pin in the center column.

STEP 3 Now, stretch a purple band from that center pin to the pin directly to the right. This is actually following the Basic Pattern, but it looks different because the loom is square.

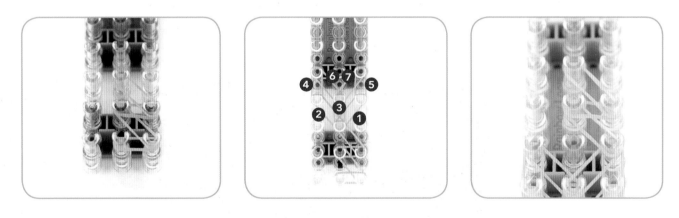

STEP 4 Place one more purple band in the Basic Pattern, going diagonally to the center column.

STEP 5 To make a heart, use pink rubber bands in the pattern and order shown in the image.

STEP 6 Now, coming from the top right point of the heart, continue the Basic Pattern with three purple bands as shown.

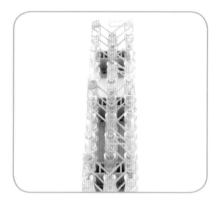

STEP 7 Continue to follow this pattern of heart section followed by Basic Pattern until you reach the end of the loom. You should be able to fit three heart sections on one loom. (To add more and make the jewelry longer, simply attach another loom to the end.)

STEP 8 Place a final purple band from the top right point of the last heart to the center pin directly to the left.

STEP 9 Finally, place a pink triple-cap band on the top left corner of each heart section as shown. It should be the corner of each heart section that doesn't touch the purple Basic Pattern bands. If you used one loom, you should have three cap bands.

LOOPING

STEP 1 Turn the loom around so that the open sides of the loom pins are facing you. Starting with the bottom left pin, loop the second-to-the-bottom pink band onto the pin where it started.

STEP 2 Going back to the same bottom left pin, loop the bottom pink band onto the pin where it started as shown.

STEP 3 Now, moving to the cap band corner of the heart, loop the second-to-the-bottom band onto its original pin.

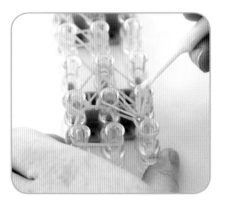

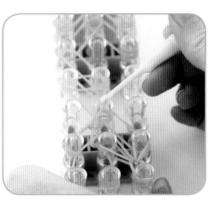

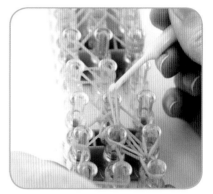

STEP 4 Back at the cap band corner, loop the remaining bottom band onto its original pin.

STEP 5 Moving to the left-hand column on the second pin up from the bottom, loop the bottom band back to its original pin.

STEP 6 Likewise, moving to the center column pin on the second pin up from the bottom, loop the bottom band back to its original pin. Then loop the band from the right-hand column back to its original pin as well.

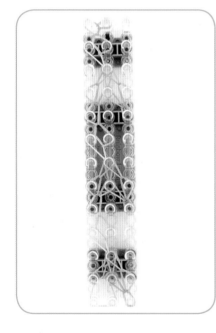

STEP 7 Loop the Basic Pattern section. At the next heart section, repeat steps 1–6. Continue this pattern to the end of the loom, remembering to loop the top band first if there are two bottom bands to loop on a particular pin. When you reach the end, finish with a Basic Extension.

Now you have a beautiful bracelet with three mini hearts to remind you to be kind to others.

TIP: Attach looms end to end to make more heart sections for your bracelet or to make a necklace.

EXTRA!

YOU CAN ALSO use the Heart or Love charms from the Bible Charms Pack when making any of these items if you follow the instructions in the EXTRA! section on page 3.

ONE WITH GOD

WE ARE TAUGHT in the Bible that God the Father, God the Son, and God the Holy Ghost are one in purpose and that we must become one with them—one in heart and one in soul. This design incorporates a color for each of the three members of the Godhead and weaves us with them in one heart, one soul, and one purpose. You will need five different colors for this design, so choose a color to represent these five things: (1) Heavenly Father, (2) Jesus Christ, (3) the Holy Ghost, (4) one heart and soul, and (5) one purpose.

LOADING

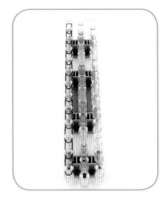

STEP 1 With the open sides of the loom pins facing away from you, place one row of rubber bands down the left column of the loom, starting at the bottom pin. Use the color you chose to represent Heavenly Father.

STEP 2 Using the color you picked for Jesus Christ, place a row of rubber bands down the center column of the loom, starting at the bottom pin as in step 1.

STEP 3 Using the color you picked for the Holy Ghost, place one row of rubber bands down the right column of the loom, starting at the bottom pin as in steps 1 and 2.

STEP 4 Using the color you chose to represent one heart and soul, place rubber bands in a diagonal pattern, going from the left pin to the center and then from the right pin to the center as shown.

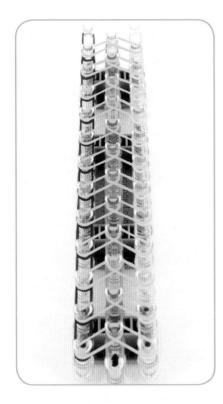

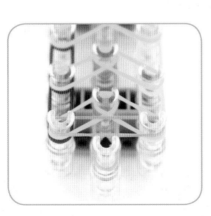

STEP 6 Using the color you chose to represent one purpose, place rubber bands straight across each row from the left column pin to the right column pin, skipping the center pin.

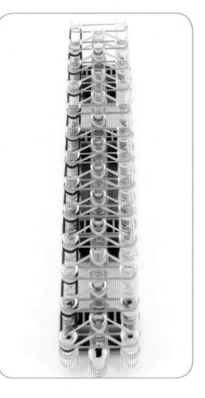

STEP 5 Continue this diagonal pattern all the way down the loom.

STEP 7 Continue this pattern all the way down the loom.

LOOPING

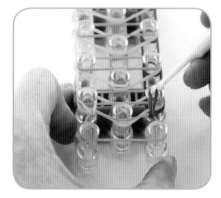

STEP 1 Turn the loom around so that the open sides of the loom pins are facing you. Start by looping the two outside bottom bands straight up onto each starting pin.

STEP 2 From the bottom center pin, loop the top band (the color for one heart and soul) diagonally onto its starting loom pin.

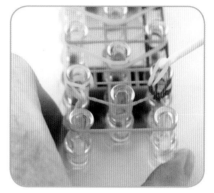

STEP 3 Going back to the bottom center pin, loop the next band (also the color for one heart and soul) diagonally onto its starting loom pin.

STEP 4 Going back to the bottom center pin once again, loop the bottom band (the color for Jesus Christ) straight up onto its starting loom pin.

STEP 5 From the second-to-the-bottom pin in the left column, loop the bottom band (the color for the Holy Ghost) straight up onto its starting loom pin.

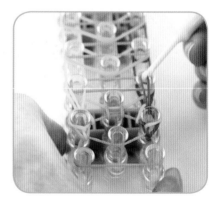

STEP 6 From the second-to-the-bottom pin in the right-hand column, loop the bottom band (the color for Heavenly Father) straight up onto its starting loom pin.

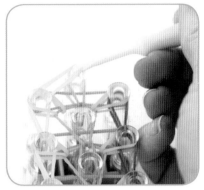

STEP 7 From the second-to-the-bottom pin in the center column, repeat steps 2–4 to loop the three bands from this pin. Then repeat steps 5 and 6 on the right- and left-hand pins next to this center pin.

STEP 8 Continue this pattern to the end of the loom, looping the inside column bands, then the outside column bands, and then moving up to the next horizontal row of pins. (Bands of the color used to represent one purpose are not looped at all.)

STEP 9 After you've finished looping, on the top pin in the left column, pull a new band of the color representing the Holy Ghost through all the bands that are looped around that top pin. Loop both ends of the new band to the top center column pin as shown.

STEP 10 Repeat step 9 on the top right pin using the color you chose to represent Heavenly Father.

STEP 11 EITHER repeat step 9 on the top center pin using the color you chose for Jesus Christ and attach a C- or S-clip to that band before slowly pulling off the bracelet, OR add a Basic Extension.

STICK OF JUDAH AND STICK OF JOSEPH

GOD TELLS US that the stick of Judah and the stick of Joseph should be used as one. The "stick" is the words written down by the lineage of Judah or the lineage of Joseph. These two written works come to us as scripture and are to be used as one. In this pattern, you will be joining two colors, each one representing the stick of Judah or the stick of Joseph, to get one fun design. The setup for this design intertwines two Basic Patterns on the right and left sides of the loom.

LOADING

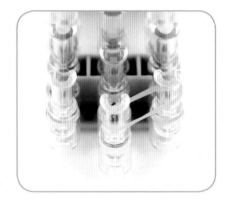

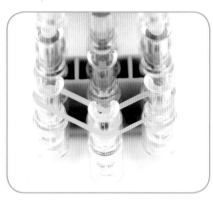

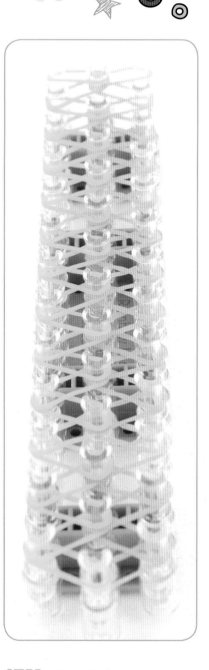

STEP 1 With the open sides of the loom pins facing away from you, stretch a purple band from the bottom center pin to the bottom right pin.

STEP 2 Stretch a green band from the bottom center pin to the bottom left pin.

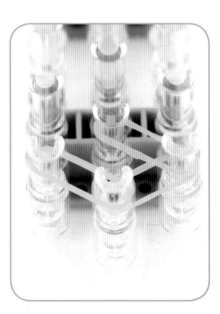

STEP 3 Place a purple band stretching from the bottom right column pin to the second pin from the bottom in the center column.

STEP 4 Place a green band stretching from the bottom left column pin to the second pin from the bottom in the center column.

STEP 5 Follow this pattern (which is same as two Basic Patterns) all the way to the end of the loom, remembering to place the purple band first in each row as shown in the picture.

LOOPING

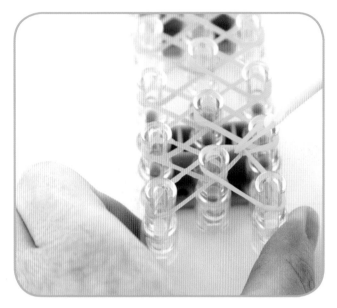

STEP 1 To start looping, turn the loom around so that the open sides of the pins are facing you. Then, starting with the bottom center pin, loop the second-to-the-bottom band (the green one) onto its starting pin.

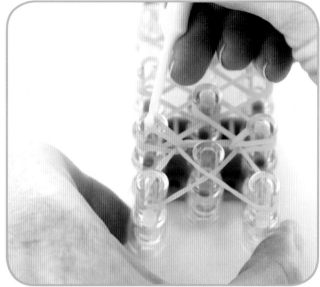

STEP 2 Also at the bottom center pin, loop the bottom band (the purple one) onto its starting pin.

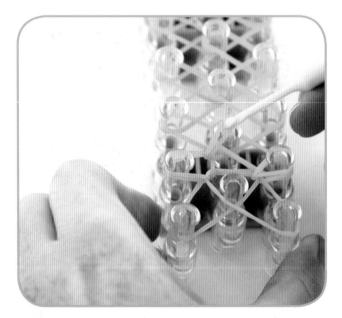

STEP 3 From the second-to-the-bottom pin in the left column, loop the purple band onto the center column pin where it started.

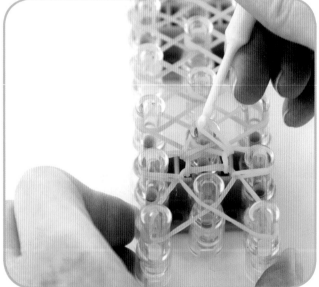

STEP 4 From the second-to-the-bottom pin in the right column, loop the green band onto the center column pin where it started.

STEP 6 When you get to the end, use another green or purple band to loop through all the bands on the top center column pin. Then attach a C- or S-clip and slowly pull the bands off the loom. Now you have your two "sticks" beautifully intertwined together.

TIP: By adding more loom columns to the right or left side of a regular three-column loom, you can intertwine more Basic Patterns to make a wider and more colorful bracelet.

STEP 5 Continue following steps 1–4, climbing your way to the top of the loom. Remember, when looping from the center column pins, loop the second-to-the-bottom band (the green one) BEFORE looping the bottom band (the purple one), but when looping the outside columns, loop the left column band (the purple one) before the right column band (the green one). This will make the bands alternate colors from top to bottom along the center column.

ABOUT THE AUTHOR

KATREINA EDEN grew up in the Midwest but eventually landed in California, where she went to law school and then ran her own law firm for a number of years. She currently works as the Executive Vice President of Cedar Fort, Inc., in Springville, Utah. Katreina also owns and operates Organiwic, LLC, an all-natural candle company, with her sister. She enjoys being out in nature and spending time with family. Aside from being published in various legal journals, this is Katreina's first trade publication.

FOR ADDED FUN, purchase the Bible Charms pack, which has charms that go with many of these designs.